CAREER PLANNER
... take your next steps with confidence ©

12-month Career Planner designed to support your decision making to your next professional experience.

Copyright 2021 by Denise Meade-Hill

All rights reserved to Denise Meade-Hill
as the identified author and designer of this book.
No part of this publication may be reproduced or stored in
a retrieval system, or transmitted, in any form or by any means,
without the prior permission of the publisher.

Published by
Transitions Career Management and Training

Design: Denise Meade-Hill

Acknowledgement

For Mum and Dad who taught me the value of Faith and hard work.

For Renae and Ethan who are beginning their life journeys.

"Start where you are. Use what you have. Do what you can."
DMH

Contents:

- **04** Introduction
- **06** Career Plan Template
- **08** You can do it!
- **12** Begin it!
- **16** Values and Interests
- **20** Clarity and Insight
- **24** Goal Setting
- **28** Transferable Skills
- **32** Your Portfolio
- **36** Resources and Support
- **40** Review
- **44** Action Plans
- **92** Be You!
- **96** Congratulations
- **98** About the Author

Introduction

If you're reading this planner, I'd say that you want more from your career and that you are prepared to do something about it! Career planning should be an integral part of your work life as the professional landscape is constantly changing and requires ongoing re-assessment to stay relevant. As with other aspects of life, having a plan helps with defining goals, getting clarity and equips you with the focus and discipline needed to take the next steps confidently.

As you go through this planner, it will be a time of discovery, while you assess your values, interests, motivations and strengths. The easy-step exercises will help you with understanding yourself better and making decisions on what you want from your role, profession or industry of your choice.

This book incorporates my experience of successfully working with coachees who have made their career transitions and it is intended to help you get started on your journey of career exploration. Careers are not static and require individuals to be able to adapt to the challenges and changes they face. This means being proactive in designing your career direction and taking ownership of the outcomes you seek.

In each section of the book there are prompts to capture your reflections, thoughts and ideas. The blank notes pages invites you to attach or draw pictures, or write reminder notes as you list your 'to do' activities. The action plan pages summarise those activities that you will prioritise and complete within a set time. Each exercise is personalised to you and can be completed in your own time frame, according to your set goal and expected gains.

This planner will form your personal guide to the career you want. Be open to the possibilities that emerge as you begin this exploratory journey and, remember to enjoy the experience!

"Higher expectations drive higher results." DMH

This planner belongs to:

Name:

Email:

Tel:

Date: _ _ / _ _ / _ _ _ _

"Start shaping the tomorrow you want, today!"
DMH

DATE

career plan ©

Where am I now?

What do I want to do next?

What are my values and interests?

What are my transferable skills?

What options are available to me?

NOTES
Add your notes, pictures and reminders here:

"The most courageous act is still to think for yourself. Aloud."
Coco Chanel

YOU CAN DO IT!

If you are here you have already taken a huge step toward getting your plan started. Affirmations are a wonderful way to remind yourself daily of your capacity to succeed. They help you to be intentional in your actions, equip you to manage unexpected bumps and twists along the way, and provide the fuel to embrace change. Here are some prompts to get you started.

Tip: *Imagine your future self when you achieve your goal*

- **Today is a good day to start working toward my goal.**

- **My dreams are valid and I can achieve all that I put my mind to.**

- **I have all the resources that I need to succeed.**

- **I will listen to my soul and be guided by it in all my interactions.**

- **I am fearless and my goals are within my reach.**

- **I am courageous and can face all that comes my way today.**

YOU CAN DO IT!

Select your favourite affirmations and add them here.
- choose short positive statements
- write them in the present tense
- repeat them to yourself every day

"I will keep the horizon in view, there are no limits there."
DMH

NOTES
Add your notes, pictures and reminders here:

"Pursue your passion and you'll never work a day in your life."
DMH

NOTES
Add your notes, pictures and reminders here:

"You don't get what you wish for, you get what you work for."
Michelle Obama

BEGIN!

Any change begins with an assessment of who you are and your vision for your life, which enables you to clarify what you want. Consider whether you are living your values and fulfilling your potential for growth. As stated in the best selling book **Start with Why** by Simon Sinek, knowing your 'why' and adopting a positive approach to life will increase your chances of success with any change you pursue. When you know your reason for this change and then start working towards your goal, you're more likely to persist, focus and make it happen. Starting with a positive outlook helps to frame your approach to getting your plan underway.

List 5 words below that describes you in a positive way:

"No pessimist ever discovered the secrets to the stars"
Helen Keller

BEGIN!

You may be looking for a new job, a new role or thinking about pursuing your dream of self-employment. It's essential to be clear about the change you are working towards, for example, changing employer, changing career direction, or changing location.

Consider the questions below:

Why are you seeking this change?

What do you want from your new role?

What motivates you?

What does success look like to you?

> "You become who you believe."
> Oprah

NOTES
Add your notes, pictures and reminders here:

"The journey of a thousand miles begins with a single step."
Chinese proverb

NOTES
Add your notes, pictures and reminders here:

"If we wait until we're ready, we never do anything."
Eleanor Roosevelt

VALUES AND INTERESTS

Values tend to be those factors that are foundational to who you are and how you interact with others. They define what's important to you and help you to set out what you really want to get out of work or life in general. Knowing your values also helps you to decide how to pursue your goals. Your interests are the things that you enjoy, which motivate you and keep you focused. These are unique to you and may consist of hobbies, leisure activities or voluntary work. The skills you use in these activities may be relevant to your new job opportunity. Complete the exercise overleaf and consider what you enjoy doing, or feel strongly about.

Values:

Interests:

"You are everything you choose to be." DMH

VALUES AND INTERESTS

List those values and interests which are most important to you and which will have the most impact on what you want to achieve from your next professional experience. Write as many as you can think of and consider how they can help you toward your goals.

Examples: Security, Independence, Money, Variety, Flexibility, Lifestyle, Influence, Status, Creativity, Socialising, Fun, Sports

"I gave my all for the things I valued."
DMH

NOTES
Add your notes, pictures and reminders here:

"Life has no limitations, except the ones you make."
Les Brown

NOTES
Add your notes, pictures and reminders here:

"The secret of your success is found in your daily routine."
John C. Maxwell

CLARITY AND INSIGHT

It's important to know yourself and to be clear about what you want to achieve. This period in your life may be one of significant change, requiring you to let go of the old way of doing things as you move into your new beginning.

To kickstart your job search or self-employment goals, you will need to conduct your research into the job market or identify the business need for your product or service. Knowing your Strengths will help you to define who you are, what you are good at and identify where you may need to address any gaps to help you achieve your goal.

Complete the Strengths Profile assessment exercise on the next page. Summarise what you have discovered about yourself and use it to build your action plan.

 What has your research revealed that you will include in your Action Plan?

"It always seems impossible until it's done."
Nelson Mandela

CLARITY AND INSIGHT
Complete the Strengths Profile assessment using the QR code

- List your top 3 realised strengths, these are the combination of skills you excel at.

- List your top 3 unrealised strengths, these are your potential for growth.

- What are the potential opportunities available to you to use your Strengths?

"You have to find what sparks a light in you so that you in your own way can illuminate the world." Oprah

NOTES

Add your notes, pictures and reminders here:

"Step out of your comfort zone, no growth happens there."
DMH

NOTES
Add your notes, pictures and reminders here:

"Far away, there in the sunshine, are my highest aspirations."
Louisa May Alcott

GOAL SETTING

Setting and achieving goals gives you a sense of accomplishment and is important to your wellbeing and happiness. Your goals should set out what you are working towards and what you genuinely want to achieve over a defined timeline. Make your goals SMART (Specific, Measurable, Achievable, Relevant, Timely). Consider what you will feel, hear, think, say and do as if you had already accomplished them.

Goal: 3-6 months

Goal: 6- 9 months

Goal: 9-12 months

"Whether you think you can or you can't, you're right" Henry Ford

GOAL SETTING

Using the goals that you set out in the previous exercise, ensure that each goal aligns with the other, so that there is a building block on each activity. Consider whether your goals reflect your values and interests.

Tip: *For each task, include an action that's exciting and memorable to keep you motivated in working on your overall goal.*

"Tune into your inner voice and listen to how capable you are."
DMH

NOTES
Add your notes, pictures and reminders here:

"Jump at de sun. You might not land on the sun but at least you will get off the ground."
Zora Neale

NOTES
Add your notes, pictures and reminders here:

"Pursue your dream. Keep focusing on making it a reality."
DMH

TRANSFERABLE SKILLS

Awareness of your skills from past or current experiences that can be applied in a new setting will help you to assess your options for personal development, job mobility or self-employment. List your key skills gained from education, home life, work experience, employment, volunteering or hobbies and see where they may fit with the goals you are working toward.

Examples: Communication, Organising, Planning, Time Management, IT skills

Tip: *Match your transferable skills with the job or business opportunity that you are considering. List them below.*

"Believe in yourself! Have faith in your abilities!"
Norman Vincent Peale

TRANSFERABLE SKILLS

Select the skills which will help you to stand out in the new job that you are seeking. Think about the context in which you used that skill and see where there may be alignment with the anticipated new experience. Consider the changing job market, the in-demand skills, and the company culture.

Tip: *Review the skills from your Strengths assessment exercise and list those that align with your goal.*

"There are no shortcuts to anywhere worth going."
Beverley Sills

NOTES
Add your notes, pictures and reminders here:

"Dig deep, discover the work for you and illuminate the world with it."
DMH

NOTES
Add your notes, pictures and reminders here:

"Shoot for the moon, because even if you miss, you'll land among the stars."
Les Brown

YOUR PORTFOLIO

Combining your personal interests with your occupational skills can help you to create a unique portfolio that brings you personal and professional satisfaction. Your portfolio may consist of skills gained from a combination of education, hobbies, volunteering, a variety of employment roles or self-employment experiences. There is no right or wrong combination of skills, only those that meet your needs and aspirations.

Tip: *Consider the pros and cons of the type of experiences that make up your portfolio and see which you would like to keep or change in your next role.*

Pros	**Cons**

"The size of your success is measured by the strength of your desire."
Robert Kiyosaki

YOUR PORTFOLIO

Consider the following questions to help you build your list of the 'pros' and 'cons' of your unique portfolio as they relate to you new career plan.

- What have been your main accomplishments to date?

- What type of job roles have you held?

- What are your personal qualities that will work for you in your new role?

- What is the demand in your industry or profession for your portfolio of skills?

"Don't let what you cannot do, stop what you can do."
DMH

NOTES
Add your notes, pictures and reminders here:

"How far do you want to go? Go the distance!"
Estee Lauder

NOTES
Add your notes, pictures and reminders here:

"Life is either a daring adventure, or nothing."
Helen Keller

RESOURCES & SUPPORT

We all need a support system to keep us going when pursuing goals. Family and friends are often great cheerleaders, they provide that emotional backing and encouragement. Colleagues and business contacts can offer professional advice and open up opportunities. A coach or mentor is like your personal guide, keeping you accountable and encouraging you to be your best self. Managing the impact of change on your time, finances, and life commitments is crucial. Create a realistic plan, set boundaries, and communicate with your support system about your priorities.

Tip: *List the names or add photos of those who can help you to achieve your goal. Outline the roles they will play in your progress.*

"Action breeds confidence and courage."
Dale Carnegie

RESOURCES & SUPPORT

Consider the following questions:

- Will you need to retrain to enter a particular role or profession?

- Do you need a financial investment to make your goal a reality?

- Have you identified individuals from your network who will support your career change?

- Are the timescales still realistic for you to reach your goal?

"Banish your apprehension, you've made it this far!"
DMH

NOTES
Add your notes, pictures and reminders here:

"If you want to go far, go together."
African Proverb

NOTES
Add your notes, pictures and reminders here:

Beware the path of least resistance!
DMH

REVIEW

Before completing your action plans, take a moment to review your progress. What have you discovered about yourself? How has your life experiences to date shaped you to be the person that you are? Has your research revealed any changes in the employment market that you need to take into account? Are there any specific areas that you will need to work on to help you achieve your goals and aspirations over the next 12 months?

Tip: *List the areas that you will need to address, below.*

"The choice is yours to make." DMH

REVIEW

Be honest in your evaluation of what you have learnt about yourself. A Wheel of Life exercise may help you to assess whether other areas of your life are in balance. Remember that your wellbeing is essential to your progress. Complete the exercise using QR code.

Scan me

- What skills and qualities have supported your progress to date?

- Are the other areas of your life in balance with the goals that you have set?

- Do you need to reconsider any aspect of your plan?

- Have you set aside a specific time to work on your Action Plan?

This is not the time to give up! DMH

NOTES
Add your notes, pictures and reminders here:

Decisions are beginnings, not endings!
DMH

NOTES
Add your notes, pictures and reminders here:

"The eagle has no fear of adversity."
Joyce Meyer

ACTION PLAN

Date: __/__/____

AFFIRMATION:

PRIORITY FOR TODAY:

Areas of Focus:
-
-
-

Which strengths or skills will you use to achieve your goal?
-
-
-

Insights: list the importance of achieving this goal
-
-
-

NOTES
Add your notes, pictures and reminders here:

"Nothing will work unless you do."
Maya Angelou

NOTES
Add your notes, pictures and reminders here:

"No pessimist ever discovered the secrets to the stars, or sailed to an unchartered land."
Helen Keller

NOTES
Add your notes, pictures and reminders here:

"You're only ever one decision away from change."
DMH

ACTION PLAN

Date: _ _/_ _/_ _ _ _

AFFIRMATION:

PRIORITY FOR TODAY:

Areas of Focus:
-
-
-

Which strengths or skills will you use to achieve your goal?
-
-
-

Insights: list the importance of achieving this goal
-
-
-

NOTES
Add your notes, pictures and reminders here:

"Life expands or shrinks in proportion to one's courage."
Anais Nin

NOTES
Add your notes, pictures and reminders here:

"It's a calamity not to dream."
Benjamin Mays

NOTES
Add your notes, pictures and reminders here:

"Willpower builds a wall of immunity against negative influences."
DMH

ACTION PLAN

Date: _ _/_ _/_ _ _ _

AFFIRMATION:

PRIORITY FOR TODAY:

Areas of Focus:
-
-
-

Which strengths or skills will you use to achieve your goal?
-
-
-

Insights: list the importance of achieving this goal
-
-
-

NOTES
Add your notes, pictures and reminders here:

"You don't need a new day to start over, you only need a new mindset."
DMH

NOTES
Add your notes, pictures and reminders here:

"Be resolute!"
DMH

NOTES
Add your notes, pictures and reminders here:

"Keep advancing, do not stop"
DMH

ACTION PLAN

Date: __/__/____

AFFIRMATION:

PRIORITY FOR TODAY:

Areas of Focus:
-
-
-

Which strengths or skills will you use to achieve your goal?
-
-
-

Insights: list the importance of achieving this goal
-
-
-

NOTES
Add your notes, pictures and reminders here:

"Faith and an optimistic attitude make all things possible."
DMH

NOTES
Add your notes, pictures and reminders here:

"Nothing can dim the light that shines from within."
Maya Angelou

NOTES
Add your notes, pictures and reminders here:

"Embrace your uniqueness. You are different, your gift is special, own it and unapologetically share it with the world."
Oprah

ACTION PLAN

Date: _ _/_ _/_ _ _ _

AFFIRMATION:

PRIORITY FOR TODAY:

Areas of Focus:
-
-
-

Which strengths or skills will you use to achieve your goal?
-
-
-

Insights: list the importance of achieving this goal
-
-
-

NOTES
Add your notes, pictures and reminders here:

"Life loves to be taken by the lapels and told, I'm with you kid. Let's go."
Maya Angelou

NOTES
Add your notes, pictures and reminders here:

"Begin to live as though your prayers are already answered."
DMH

NOTES
Add your notes, pictures and reminders here:

"Starve your distractions, feed your focus."
DMH

ACTION PLAN

Date: __/__/____

AFFIRMATION:

PRIORITY FOR TODAY:

Areas of Focus:
-
-
-

Which strengths or skills will you use to achieve your goal?
-
-
-

Insights: list the importance of achieving this goal
-
-
-

NOTES
Add your notes, pictures and reminders here:

"Every great dream begins with a dreamer."
Harriet Tubman

NOTES
Add your notes, pictures and reminders here:

" A little progress each day adds up to big results."
DMH

NOTES
Add your notes, pictures and reminders here:

"The greatest enemy of direction is distraction."
Dennis Greenidge

ACTION PLAN

Date: __/__/____

AFFIRMATION:

PRIORITY FOR TODAY:

Areas of Focus:
-
-
-

Which strengths or skills will you use to achieve your goal?
-
-
-

Insights: list the importance of achieving this goal
-
-
-

NOTES
Add your notes, pictures and reminders here:

"When the why is clear, the how is easy."
Viktor E Frankl

NOTES
Add your notes, pictures and reminders here:

"No one else is you, and that is your super power."
DMH

NOTES
Add your notes, pictures and reminders here:

"Don't stop shining because someone is intimidated by your light."
Lisa Nichols

ACTION PLAN

Date: __/__/____

AFFIRMATION:

PRIORITY FOR TODAY:

Areas of Focus:
-
-
-

Which strengths or skills will you use to achieve your goal?
-
-
-

Insights: list the importance of achieving this goal
-
-
-

NOTES
Add your notes, pictures and reminders here:

"As long as you are able to draw breath in this universe, you have a chance."
Cicely Tyson

NOTES
Add your notes, pictures and reminders here:

"It always seems impossible until it's done."
Nelson Mandela

NOTES
Add your notes, pictures and reminders here:

"Consistency is more important than perfection."
DMH

ACTION PLAN

Date: __/__/____

AFFIRMATION:

PRIORITY FOR TODAY:

Areas of Focus:
-
-
-

Which strengths or skills will you use to achieve your goal?
-
-
-

Insights: list the importance of achieving this goal
-
-
-

NOTES
Add your notes, pictures and reminders here:

"I am the sole judge and jury of what my limits will be."
Gloria Naylor

NOTES
Add your notes, pictures and reminders here:

"It's never too late for a new beginning in your life."
Joyce Meyer

NOTES
Add your notes, pictures and reminders here:

"Don't forget to be awesome."
DMH

ACTION PLAN

Date: __/__/____

AFFIRMATION:

PRIORITY FOR TODAY:

Areas of Focus:
-
-
-

Which strengths or skills will you use to achieve your goal?
-
-
-

Insights: list the importance of achieving this goal
-
-
-

NOTES
Add your notes, pictures and reminders here:

"Willpower is like a muscle, the more you train it, the stronger it gets."
DMH

NOTES
Add your notes, pictures and reminders here:

"There is growth on the other side of fear."
Michelle Obama

NOTES
Add your notes, pictures and reminders here:

"Where focus goes, energy flows."
Tony Robbins

ACTION PLAN

Date: __/__/____

AFFIRMATION:

PRIORITY FOR TODAY:

Areas of Focus:
-
-
-

Which strengths or skills will you use to achieve your goal?
-
-
-

Insights: list the importance of achieving this goal
-
-
-

NOTES
Add your notes, pictures and reminders here:

"Nothing is impossible, the word itself says, I'm possible."
Audrey Hepburn

NOTES
Add your notes, pictures and reminders here:

"You are what you do, not what you say you will do."
DMH

NOTES
Add your notes, pictures and reminders here:

"You miss 100% of the shots you don't take."
Wayne Gretzky

ACTION PLAN

Date: __/__/____

AFFIRMATION:

PRIORITY FOR TODAY:

Areas of Focus:
-
-
-

Which strengths or skills will you use to achieve your goal?
-
-
-

Insights: list the importance of achieving this goal
-
-
-

NOTES
Add your notes, pictures and reminders here:

"Believe in yourself. Have Faith in your abilities"
Norman Vincent Peale

NOTES
Add your notes, pictures and reminders here:

"If you don't like something, change it. If you can't change it change your attitude."
Maya Angelou

NOTES
Add your notes, pictures and reminders here:

"You cannot have a positive life and a negative mind."
Joyce Meyer

BE YOU!

We all have a unique contribution to make in this world. Don't stay stuck in an environment or role that doesn't allow you to shine. As you carve your career pathway, live true to your values, believe in yourself and tell your story in your own way. Step forward in confidence with a positive perspective, an optimistic attitude and a growth mindset to make your goals a reality!

Tip: *Commit to working on 3 things from your Action Plan. List them below.*

"Remember to enjoy the journey of self-discovery"
DMH

BE YOU!

Your career plan should incorporate elements that provide you with personal and professional satisfaction and enable you to feel a sense of accomplishment.

- Are you considering jobs and roles in the right working environment for you?

- Do the roles have the right level of responsibility or challenge for you?

- In what way will the job tasks make the most of your skills and abilities?

- What are your motivators for choosing your role of interest?

> "We were born to make manifest the glory of God that is within us. It's not just in some of us, it's in everyone."
> Marianne Williamson

NOTES
Add your notes, pictures and reminders here:

"You are responsible for maintaining your energy. It's your goal!"
DMH

NOTES
Add your notes, pictures and reminders here:

"Persistence is one of the keys to success."
DMH

CONGRATULATIONS

You have taken the first step in your development by completing your career planning journey. Take some time to *reflect* on what you have discovered about yourself along the way and embrace the new you. To build on your career plan, book your 1:1 accountability session with me.

Scan me

To do:

"If you can get the courage to begin, you have the courage to succeed."
David Viscott

NOTES
Add your notes, pictures and reminders here:

"Dreams do not come true just because you've dreamed them.
It's hard work that creates change."
Shonda Rhimes

About the Author:

Denise Meade-Hill is a Career Transition Coach who specialises in career change, whether self-directed or imposed through external factors, e.g. taking a career break, career repositioning or a redundancy.

She is passionate about enabling individuals to be active participants in their professional lives, through identifying their strengths and developing the self-belief to fulfil their potential. Her experience spans the public, private and not-for-profit sectors, where she has supported employability programmes and coached employees through organisational change as they transition into new roles.

Denise is a Registered Career Development Professional with the Career Development Institute and an accredited EMCC Senior Practitioner Coach. Her approach to coaching is underpinned by her knowledge of Positive Psychology and she is a Strengths Profile Practitioner with Cappfinity.

Contact:
Website: www.careertransitionsdmh.co.uk
LinkedIn: www.linkedin.com/in/denisemeadehill
Facebook / Twitter: @TransitionsDMH
Instagram denisemeadehill_careercoach

"We can all change, grow and progress through effort, application and experience."

www.ingramcontent.com/pod-product-compliance
Lightning Source LLC
Chambersburg PA
CBHW071408080526
44587CB00017B/3218